Contents

¡Hola!

Me llamo Daniel.

My name is Daniel.

World Languages

Families in
Spanish

Daniel Nunn

Raintree is an imprint of Capstone Global Library Limited, a company incorporated in England and Wales having its registered office at 7 Pilgrim Street, London, EC4V 6LB – Registered company number: 6695582

www.raintreepublishers.co.uk
myorders@raintreepublishers.co.uk

Text © Capstone Global Library Limited 2013
First published in hardback in 2013
First published in paperback in 2014
The moral rights of the proprietor have been asserted.

Edited by Daniel Nunn, Rebecca Rissman & Sian Smith
Designed by Joanna Hinton-Malivoire
Picture research by Tracy Cummins
Production by Victoria Fitzgerald
Originated by Capstone Global Library Ltd
Printed and bound in China by Leo Paper Products Ltd

ISBN 978 1 406 25086 2 (hardback)
16 15 14 13 12
10 9 8 7 6 5 4 3 2 1

ISBN 978 1 406 25093 0 (paperback)
17 16 15 14 13
10 9 8 7 6 5 4 3 2 1

British Library Cataloguing in Publication Data

Nunn, Daniel.
Families in Spanish: las familias. – (World languages. Families)
1. Spanish language–Vocabulary–Pictorial works–Juvenile literature. 2. Families–Spain–Terminology–Pictorial works–Juvenile literature.
I. Title II. Series
468.1-dc23

Acknowledgements

We would like to thank the following for permission to reproduce photographs: Shutterstock pp.4 (Catalin Petolea), 5 (optimarc), 5, 6 (Petrenko Andriy), 5, 7 (Tyler Olson), 5, 8 (Andrey Shadrin), 9 (Erika Cross), 10 (Alena Brozova), 5, 11 (Maxim Petrichuk), 12 (auremar), 13 (Mika Heittola), 5, 14, 15 (Alexander Raths), 5, 16 (Samuel Borges), 17 (Vitalii Nesterchuk), 18 (pat138241), 19 (Fotokostic), 20 (Cheryl Casey), 21 (spotmatik).

Cover photographs of two women and a man reproduced with permission of Shutterstock (Yuri Arcurs). Cover photograph of a girl reproduced with permission of istockphoto (© Sean Lockes). Back cover photograph of a girl reproduced with permission of Shutterstock (Erika Cross).

We would like to thank Rebeca Otazua Bideganeta for her invaluable help in the preparation of this book.

Every effort has been made to contact copyright holders of material reproduced in this book. Any omissions will be rectified in subsequent printings if notice is given to the publisher.

Y ésta es mi familia.

And this is my family.

Mi madre y mi padre

mi madre

Ésta es mi madre.

This is my mother.

mi padre

Éste es mi padre.

This is my father.

Mi hermano y mi hermana

mi hermano

Éste es mi hermano.

This is my brother.

mi hermana

Ésta es mi hermana.

This is my sister.

Mi madrastra y mi padrastro

mi madrastra

Ésta es mi madrastra.

This is my step-mother.

Éste es mi padrastro.

This is my step-father.

Mi hermanastro y mi hermanastra

mi hermanastro

Éste es mi hermanastro.

This is my step-brother.

mi hermanastra

Ésta es mi hermanastra.

This is my step-sister.

Mi abuela y mi abuelo

mi abuela

Ésta es mi abuela.

This is my grandmother.

Éste es mi abuelo.

This is my grandfather.

Mi tía y mi tío

mi tía

Ésta es mi tía.

This is my aunt.

mi tío

Éste es mi tío.

This is my uncle.

Mis primos

mi prima

Éstos son mis primos.

These are my cousins.

mi primo

Mis amigos

mi amiga

Éstos son mis amigos.

These are my friends.

Dictionary

Spanish word	How to say it	English word
abuela	a-bue-la	grandmother
abuelo	a-bue-lo	grandfather
amiga	a-mee-ga	friend (female)
amigo	a-mee-go	friend (male)
amigos	a-mee-gos	friends
es	es	is
ésta	es-ta	this (female)
éste	es-te	this (male)
éstos	es-tos	these
familia	fa-mee-lee-a	family
hermana	er-maa-na	sister
hermanastra	er-maa-nas-tra	step-sister
hermanastro	er-maa-nas-tro	step-brother
hermano	er-maa-no	brother
hola	o-la	hello
madrastra	maa-dras-tra	step-mother

Spanish word	How to say it	English word
madre	maa-dre	mother
me llamo	me ya-mo	my name is
mi	mee	my (singular)
mis	mees	my (plural)
padrastro	paa-dras-tro	step-father
padre	paa-dre	father
prima	pree-ma	cousin (female)
primo	pree-mo	cousin (male)
primos	pree-mos	cousins
son	sohn	are
tía	tee-a	aunt
tío	tee-o	uncle
y	ee	and

See words in the "How to say it" columns for a rough guide to pronunciations.

Index

Notes for parents and teachers

In Spanish, nouns are either masculine or feminine. The word for 'this' changes accordingly – either 'éste' (masculine) or 'ésta' (feminine). The Spanish word for 'these' used on pages 18 and 20 is 'éstos', which is the masculine plural. The feminine plural used to describe two or more female cousins or friends would be 'éstas'.

Sometimes nouns have different spellings too, which is why the word for 'cousin' can be spelled either 'primo' (male) or 'prima' (female), and the word for 'friend' can be spelled either 'amigo' or 'amiga'. The masculine plurals 'primos' and 'amigos' are used to describe a mixed group. The feminine plurals used to decribe female cousins or friends would be 'primas' or 'amigas'.